The Florida Parent's Divorce Handbook:

How to Protect Your Rights, So You Can Protect Your Kids

First Edition

By Alexander C. Peterson, Esquire

Family First Legal Group

TABLE OF CONTENTS

Introduction..1

Section One: Parenting While Going Through a Divorce 5

Section Two: The Florida Parent's Survival Guide to Divorce..15

Section Three: Essential Information about the Florida Divorce Process 25

Section Four: How to Select the Right Family Law Attorney for Your Needs 51

Conclusion 61

Disclaimer..63

INTRODUCTION

Why did we divorce? I guess you could say we had trouble synchronizing. You know that carnival ride where two cages swing in opposite directions, going higher and higher until they go over the top? That was us. We passed each other all the time, but we never actually stopped in the same place until it was time to get off the ride.

– Diane Hammond, *Hannah's Dream*

Divorce creates tremendous challenges, even when both spouses conduct themselves ethically, mindfully work to negotiate mutually beneficial solutions, protect the best interests of the children, and engage the process methodically. Conflicts between parents, unexpected surprises, and stresses unrelated to the separation itself can all make the process much more complicated and painful.

Whether you and your spouse separated after months of discussions and therapy, or you discovered that your partner had been having an affair, the marriage is over, and the relationship is beyond reconciliation. Given that you have children together, you need to take positive, concrete actions to protect their rights and well being and to ensure your own autonomy. Divorce creates vulnerabilities for children, psychologically and emotionally, and ratchets up the normal, chronic stresses of parenthood.

Given these unpleasant realities, what can a caring parent like you do? How can you divorce with dignity and assist your children through this transition?

This book provides a detailed answer to those two pivotal questions. While it should not be construed as legal advice, it will teach you how to think constructively about the divorce, how to approach your impending court battles well-prepared and supported by an effective strategy, and how to pick up the pieces, so you and your children can rebuild.

Here are the topics we will be covering in the chapters to follow:

Section One: Parenting While Going Through a Divorce

We will systematically address the biggest challenges parents face regarding managing their children, negotiating with co-parents, dealing with outbursts and other natural emotional reactions, and other topics of concern.

Section Two: The Florida Parent's Survival Guide

We have compiled a comprehensive catalogue of local organizations, articles and other resources to help you meet diverse challenges, ranging from scheduling visits to obtaining therapy for Parental Alienation. Other issues we will cover will include: ADHD; anger; insomnia and school bullying. We will also address parental concerns, such as: dating, budgeting, logistics, addiction, grocery shopping, exercise, rethinking your career, and raising your kids so that they become happy, well-adjusted adults.

Section Three: Essential Information about the Florida Divorce Process

This section will introduce important legal ideas and terminology, so you can advocate for your rights resourcefully. It will also discuss what makes litigated divorces with children distinct from other types of divorces and explain how to approach your situation strategically.

Section Four: How to Select the Right Family Law Attorney for Your Needs

Given the constellation of potential law firms who might be able to serve you, what decision making criteria will be most resourceful? Once you do find a match, what can you do to work effectively with that law firm?

We hope that this book helps you navigate the challenges ahead effectively. For a confidential case evaluation, call our team at the Family First Legal Group at (239) 206-3664, or explore more resources about parenting and divorce at www.familyfirstlegalgroup.com.

SECTION ONE

PARENTING WHILE GOING THROUGH A DIVORCE

Before I got married I had six theories about raising children; now, I have six children and no theories.

- John Wilmot, 2nd Earl of Rochester (1647-1680)

One of your main priorities involves minimizing the impact of your separation on your children. Frustratingly and unknowingly, however, many parents make significant mistakes during the process that have negative impacts on the ones they love most. Below, we have compiled critical lessons about how to become more aware of your children's needs during the process and to get through the transition.

To develop the following list of tips, we sought contributions and insights from South Florida's preeminent child psychologists, family counselors and parenting coordinators.

1. Live the Golden Rule, and support the other parent's relationship with your children.

Your former spouse may have engaged in dubious, hurtful or even genuinely destructive behavior that either caused or hastened the separation. However, to the extent that doing so would not expose your children to risk or alienation, strive to move beyond your own emotional pain, and enourage your children to develop strong relationships with the other parent. Identify the positives in your ex's ability to parent, and avoid petty criticism or scorekeeping. Engage this process not necessarily to win favors from the other parent but rather as a genuine act of altruism.

2. Avoid overcompensating or trying to win favor from your children.

Your children need to see you as a parent, not as a friend. Don't use your break up as an excuse to cater to your children or to view your children on some sliding scale to try to garner more "love."

Along these lines, avoid incorporating your child into any litigation. Don't involve your children in issues that are outside of their control. They want to see problems resolved; frustratingly for them, however, they lack the means to fix them. For the same reasons we don't trouble our children with our financial or work problems, keep them out of your divorce process.

Appreciate that, when your children feel alone, tired, confused and angry about the divorce, you may experience powerful emotions of your own in response. What caring parent wouldn't want to ameliorate that kind of pain in their children? Rather than respond to the children's immediate wants and desires (e.g. requests for meals out or toys you cannot afford), react with openness and empathy. Acknowledge what your children are experiencing, and allow them to "feel felt" by you.

For an excellent system for empathetically communicating with children during turbulent times, explore the resources at the Center for Non Violent Communication, cnvc.org.

3. Understand that children will align more with the parent of the same gender during certain stages of development.

Fathers need to know that daughters will align with their mothers as their bodies grow and change, and vice versa. Do not take this developmental response personally.

4. Don't speak negatively about the other parent in front of the children, and reduce the level of conflict (including non-verbal conflict) that they see or experience.

Always be mindful that your children are watching you. If you are in the front yard having a heated conversation while flailing your arms and yelling into the phone, your children will see you through the window. Carrying the conflict on your shoulders all day can have a profound impact on children. Maintaining your composure in front of your children will increase their personal self-worth and self-esteem. Remind yourself to avoid carrying negative emotions around, and get therapy if you need it.

5. Strive for consistency between both households.

If the joint home had certain bedtime or other rituals, it will benefit the transitioning child to experience the same rituals in the new home. The rituals do not have to be identical, but the more consistency between homes, the better for the child.

6. Don't hold onto anger and resentment.

The break up of your family unit isn't the beginning of the turmoil in your relationship, and it will not be the end, but it can be the *beginning* of the end. Make it a point to remind yourself not to carry negative emotions around. Stress can have debilitating psychological as well as physiological consequences, causing health problems, such as obesity and hypertension. Don't let that happen to you!

7. Let your children know it isn't their fault.

Often times children – especially adolescent children – carry around guilt and blame themselves for the failure of their parents' marriage. Do your best to consistently and lovingly remind them that it is not their fault and that you and your ex's love for them has never and will never change.

8. Avoid neglecting your children.

Often children will tell you they miss you even when you're there with them after a breakup. They do this not for attention; they do this because they truly miss you. When you are away, your kids will look forward to your return. Put down your phone, and turn off Facebook and Instagram. Focus on them, and be fully present.

9. Let the children know it is okay to love and talk about the other parent in your home.

In your children's minds, when they leave your house, they think you are frozen in time, waiting for them to return. It is okay for your children to express the fact that they miss your ex. Foster that feeling, and empathize with it. Cultivate an open, accepting atmosphere, where you all can express your emotions safely and without repercussions.

Along those lines, encourage your children to call the other parent while in your care if the children miss him or her. Try to avoid monitoring these conversations. Don't put the phone on speaker and listen. This interrupts the child's ability to spend a moment with the other parent.

10. Listen to your children.

Intuitively, parents recognize that children are wise beyond their years. Respect them, and actively listen to their opinions and needs.

11. Accept the inevitability of change.

Things will never be what they were before. Change has come. For children and adults alike, uncertainty can be scary. Prepare your children. They need to know that change is here and that what is done will not be undone.

13. Just because children don't want to chat with you on the phone (or on Skype) doesn't mean they don't love you and want to see you.

As a rule, children don't love talking on the telephone. Don't expect a youngster to want to talk to you for more than a few fleeting moments. Recognize that phone calls are more for you than for them. They are still expecting you to be frozen in place anxiously awaiting their return.

14. Pick up and drop off time should be in a neutral setting; keep a distance.

As painful as it is to say goodbye to your children for an extended period of time at the exchange, encourage the children, and make it a positive experience for them. When you end your parenting time, implicitly approve what's happening with the transition. Rather than implying *Mommy or Daddy is taking you from me*, convey a more open-hearted sentiment: *I approve of this, and I love you. Have fun.*

15. Don't rush the introduction of a new significant other into a child's life.

Children need time to grieve the "loss" of a parent. Introducing a new parental figure into their lives too quickly can have a harmful impact. As the New York Times recently reported (http://nyti.ms/1KODvT3): and continue with the rest of the sentence as-is.: "Divorce and breakup can affect children badly. But parents shouldn't rush into another relationship just to provide a stable home. One study… found that every time a partner entered or left a household, the odds of an adolescent stealing, skipping school or getting drunk increased by 12 percent, though… the majority of adolescents with broken homes don't exhibit delinquent behavior."

16. Reach out for help to come up with a middle ground.

Qualified professionals can help your children grow through changes rather than simply react passively to them. Cultivate a support system, and reach out to friends, family members and other trusted figures for assistance.

17. Don't be inconsistent with your parenting techniques, even after you find a new partner.

It is very common for parents to find new partners and for those partners to seek to instill new parenting "standards" on the children. Don't allow this to happen. Remain steadfast in your parenting technique with your children.

18. Don't try to make up for five years in a weekend.

Often, as parents grow apart, one parent can become more removed from the children. If this happens to you, acknowledge your feelings and the deeper needs driving them, but don't try to make up for lost time in a weekend. There will be time for you to reestablish your relationship with your children. Take it slowly.

19. Utilize grandparents for help.

Grandparents can offer perspective on the break up and provide a safe haven for the children. Utilize them, but encourage them to avoid any discussions with the children about the break up of the family. Make it clear to your parents that you do not want any negative statements made about the other parent to, or around, the child.

20. Don't take anything personally.

You and your ex are going through the same process, but you are seeing it and experiencing it through very different lenses. Avoid taking comments or actions personally, because they merely reflect the other person's feelings and needs, not necessarily the truth or reality.

SECTION TWO

THE FLORIDA PARENT'S SURVIVAL GUIDE TO DIVORCE

Our greatest glory is not in never falling, but in rising every time we fall.

-- Confucius

Below, we have catalogued a variety of resources to help you deal with challenges pertaining to your divorce. Please click on the links directly to learn more. If you need help beyond what is listed below, you are always welcome to call our offices for insight at 239-206-3664.

General Resources for People Getting Divorced in Florida

Parent Coaching Institute (PCI), thepci.org

Many exceptional PCI certified parent coaches work with Florida parents and coach them through their difficulties and challenges. The Institute offers a wealth of resources. Here is the PCI's mission, per its website:

"The Parent Coaching Institute, a training organization, is the originator of parent coaching, setting the highest standards for parent coaching professionals. Through our innovative coaching model we energize, assist, and inspire parents, co-creating with them new levels of family fulfillment and parenting enjoyment.

An important part of our mission is to intentionally co-construct effective, evidence-based strategies with the parents we serve so they can positively impact external pressures (such as the impact of media and the high stress of today's world) that directly affect parental decisions and the home environment. In our increasingly complex society, parents have more challenges than ever. Therefore, family support must shift dramatically to adequately address these profound changes. The PCI leads the new paradigm for supporting families, effectively shifting to a living systems, synergetic model with extraordinarily positive results."

2Houses, 2houses.com

This useful site offers organizational tools to help parents communicate with one another, track their responsibilities, budget expenses and more. Per the website, some of the functionalities include:

"We help you to: **organize** your schedule and keep track of all activities, **manage** your expenses, and easily **exchange** school, after-school, and medical information..

To-do management, shopping lists, and document storage are just a few of the many **features** that 2houses offers. We are accessible via a web platform and mobile apps for **iPhone** and **Android**."

Our Family Wizard, ourfamilywizard.com

Another very practical organizing tool, this site offers ways for parents to collaborate with respect to child care and visitation logistics. Per the company's online materials: "The OurFamilyWizard website® is so effective that judges in nearly all 50 states and 5 Canadian provinces have ordered families to utilize the site in contested cases to reduce family conflict."

Some of the benefits include:

- Coordinate custody and time sharing schedules with accurate record keeping.
- Reduce the challenges of budgeting and splitting expenses.
- Make sure both parents are on the same page with respect to crucial information about the children, including their doctor's records, immunizations, school registrations, and so forth.
- Document correspondence safely and securely.

The CoParenting Took Kit, thecoparentingtoolkit.com

This short book provides a wealth of tips and strategies to make coparenting more efficient, to assert your needs, and to map out an approach that will work for everyone and protect your children.

Other Resources for Parents

Attention Deficit Hyperactivity Disorder (ADHD)

Studies suggest that ADHD affects at least 5% of all American children, and parents who have children with the disorder are substantially more likely to get divorced for reasons that reseachers are still debating.

One Study *(Divorce More Likely in ADHD Families?, WebMD.com)* found some eye-opening results: "Nearly twice as many parents of ADHD children had divorced by the time the child was age 8, the study showed. Although 22.7% of the parents with ADHD children had divorced by the time the affected child was 8, just 12.6% of parents whose children did not have ADHD had split by the time the child was 8."

What can you do as a concerned parent? Here are some useful resources:

- ADHD and Divorce, childandfamilymentalhealth.com/adhd/adhd-and-divorce

- Reducing the Impact of Divorce upon Children with ADHD, chesapeakeadd.com/#!reducing-the-impact-of-divorce-upon-chil/c166p
- ADHD or Not ADHD: Custody and Visitation Considerations, healthyparent.com/ADHD-divorce.pdf

Anger and Depression and Other Powerful Emotions

Children and parents alike experience tremendously intense feelings during divorce that must be processed carefully. Here are some articles and other resources to help you manage:

- Coping with Divorce-Related Anger, divorcemag.com/articles/coping-with-divorce-related-anger
- Divorce and Kids: Dealing with Serious Anger Issues, huffingtonpost.com/2011/08/02/kids-of-divorce_n_913153.html
- Feeling Hatred Is Normal in Divorce: Intense anger may be part of your grief process, psychologytoday.com/blog/contemplating-divorce/201105/feeling-hatred-is-normal-in-divorce
- Parental Divorce & Teen Depression, psyweb.com/articles/depression/parental-divorce-teen-depression

- Be Prepared For Emotional Mood Swings During And After Your Divorce, tipsofdivorce.com/be-prepared-for-emotional-mood-swings-during-and-after-your-divorce

School Bullying

When children move to new schools, particulary under duress, they may be extra vulnerable to peer pressure and peer derision. As a parent who's overwhelmed with your own grief, anger and logistical challenges, how should you protect your children, physically and emotionally, if you notice signs that bullying is occurring? Here are some resources:

- National Bullying Prevention Center, pacer.org/bullying/resourcesr
- StopBullying.Gov
- Kids, divorce, and school success, greatschools.org/gk/articles/kids-divorce-and-school-success

Abuse and Neglect

Whether you have personally suffered abuse during your marriage (including verbal or emotional abuse), or you need insights to help your children who have been victimized, here are some helpful resources:

- Family Resource Center of South Florida, frcflorida.org
- Florida Abuse Hotline, myflfamilies.com/service-programs/abuse-hotline
- Prevent Child Abuse Florida, ounce.org/PreventionServices.asp

Budgeting and Logistics

Especially if your ex spouse typically handled the household finances, you might be confused about how to approach logistical and money related projects. Consider the following articles and websites for insight:

- Getting Things Done, gettingthingsdone.com
- How To Budget Your Money After Divorce, divorcesupport.about.com/od/lovethenexttimearound/ht/budget_money.htm
- After the Divorce: How to Get Your Financial Feet Back, daveramsey.com/blog/after-the-divorce-get-financial-feet-back

Diet and Excercise

Most Americans are bombarded by conflicting information about how to eat and how to exercise to achieve our fitness goals. Unfortunately, the scientific debate over these topics has turned particularly rancorous in recent years, thanks to evidence that has emerged indicting much of the conventional wisdom in nutrition and fitness. In 2015, for instance, the British Medical Journal conducted an investigation (bmj.com/content/351/bmj.h4962) into the official process that determines the U.S. Dietary Guidelines and found that "the expert report underpinning the next set of US Dietary Guidelines for Americans fails to reflect much relevant scientific literature in its reviews of crucial topics and therefore risks giving a misleading picture… The omissions seem to suggest a reluctance by the committee behind the report to consider any evidence that contradicts the last 35 years of nutritional advice."

So how should parents feed themselves and exercise? How should they encourage their children to get fit?

The scientific answers to these questions are hotly debated among researchers. Two organizations are working diligently to conduct experiments to settle the debate. Please explore the following websites to learn more about the process and discussion:

- The Nutrition Coalition, nutrition-coalition.org
- The Nutrition Science Initiative, nusi.org
- The CHEK Institute, chekinstitute.com

Rethinking Your Career, Parenting and Life Goals

Establishing longer term goals for yourself and for your children is tricky, even if you are not caught up in a complex and time-consuming litigation process. That being said, the following resources can help you plan for the future, reinvestigate your career potential and reach your goals:

- Stay-at-Home Mom Facing Divorce? Don't Expect Alimony, forbes.com/sites/emmajohnson/2014/10/27/are-you-a-stay-at-home-mom-facing-divorce-dont-expect-alimony
- What Divorce Does to Your Career: How divorce can help you get a better job and reach your career goals, more.com/reinvention-money/careers/what-divorce-does-your-career
- After Divorce or Job Loss Comes the Good Identity Crisis: Experts say most people should give themselves a good two years to recover from an emotional trauma, wsj.com
- Seven Ways to Thrive After Divorce, psychologytoday.com/blog/the-intelligent-divorce/201309/seven-ways-thrive-after-divorce

SECTION THREE

ESSENTIAL INFORMATION ABOUT THE FLORIDA DIVORCE PROCESS

It's not only children who grow. Parents do, too. As much as we watch to see what our children do with their lives, they are watching us to see what we do with ours. I can't tell my children to reach for the sun. All I can do is reach for it, myself.

– Joyce Maynard

In this chapter, we will introduce key ideas, terms and rules about Florida divorce and then discuss specific concerns about divorce litigation as it relates to child custody and visitation.

An Overview of Florida Divorce

Florida permits **no-fault** divorce. This means you don't need to prove your spouse did anything wrong to end the marriage. Any person who has lived in the state for at least six months can seek a divorce in Florida. You can also file for divorce if the other person has been mentally incapacitated for a minimum of three years. The courts can finalize divorce 20 days after your spouse "defaults" or fails to file an answer in your case.

Property Division Laws

The state uses the rule of **equitable distribution**, which means that marital property should be divided equitably between both parties. The courts assume a 50 – 50 division but will consider a different ratio, depending on the following circumstances:

- The length of the marriage
- The contributions of each person
- The economic circumstances of each person
- Whether one parent will remain in the family home and
- Other relevant factors.

Alimony

The Florida courts might order temporary or permanent alimony, called **spousal support**. The **receiving spouse** must have a legitimate need for this money, while the **paying spouse** must be able to afford the payments. The court will review numerous financial and other factors, such as the resources of each party, their earning capacities, the length of the marriage and their standard of living. The courts might also consider if one person committed adultery during the marriage or engaged in other bad behavior, such as abuse, neglect or criminal conduct.

The Best Interests of the Children

Ending your marriage changes your relationship with your former partner, but you will both continue to be parents to your children.[1] If you can discuss important issues regarding your children with your soon-to-be ex outside of court, you will be establishing the needed tools to resolve differences in your children's best interests in the future. If you cannot do so, the court will have to make decisions for you, and it will make those choices based on what's in the best interest of your children from the limited information the Court receives from you, your former spouse, your respective lawyers and your witnesses.

All things being equal, Florida courts prefer children to have regular and frequent contact with both parents. Both parents have an obligation to encourage a quality relationship between the other parent and the children.

Parenting Plans

Before the state finalizes a Florida divorce, both parents must attend a live or virtual **parenting class**. In some cases, parents

1 Barring extreme circumstances. It is very rare for a parent's rights to be terminated in a Dissolution of Marriage case, and that outcome can typically only happen if someone brings a separate and distinct petition to terminate such a parent's rights.

might benefit from speaking with various professionals, including counselors, parenting facilitators, family law mediators, and family lawyers, before they put together a parenting plan.

A **parenting plan** is a comprehensive contract between you and your former spouse that should detail how you are going to co-parent your children unitl they are adults. The courts consider 20 factors when ruling on a parenting plan, some of which follow:

- Communication and cooperation of each parent
- Maintaining continuity when it comes to the home environment and schooling
- The ability and moral qualities of each parent
- The parents' overall physical and emotional health
- The child's behavior at home, in the community and at school
- The geographical logistics of the plan, especially concerning travel
- The child's physical health and safety. (The courts can order supervised visitation or a "safety-focused" parenting plan where there is neglect, abuse, abandonment, substance abuse and domestic or sexual violence.)
- Developmental and emotional needs

The parenting plan must be written out in order to be approved by the court and must detail the *at minimum* the following:

- The child's designated address
- A communication plan for both parents and ways to reach the child
- Who will handle school and health care
- How parents will share responsibility for daily tasks and
- Where the children will spend their time and with whom.

Most parenting plans are agreed upon prior to trial, and they are ordered by the court and enforceable. In rare cases, the parents will draw up a plan and agree to it, but the court will reject that plan and establish another one. In other cases, third parties can intervene if the parents cannot effectively protect the minor children. In extreme cases, the courts will specify every detail of an exchange. The courts also have the right to order a home study, and the people or agency investigating the case must provide a written summary of findings along with recommendations.

Jurisdictional Considerations

The Uniform Child Custody Jurisdiction Enforcement Act UCCJEA (uniformlaws.org), governs jurisdiction over children's issues. In simple terms, this Act says that, unless there is an emergency or other certain circumstances, the children need to be in the state for six months in order for the court to have jurisdiction over the marriage and the children. In a divorce case, these jurisdictional restrictions are quite clear, save for an emergency.

Common Mistakes Parents Make

Many parents presume that child custody and support will be divided 50-50. This is not necessarily the case. Advocates who want alimony reform have tried various strategies to do away with permanent alimony or change alimony. However, at least as of 2016, these attempts at alimony reform in Florida have not succeeded for various political and logistical reasons.

This reality notwithstanding, many parents mistakenly operate under the assumption that parents are automatically entitled to 50-50.

Many Florida parents also incorrectly believe that it is possible to predict the outcome in child custody disputes. No amount of experience or advance information can lead to accurate forecasting. Too many unknowns come into play regarding variables like the judge's disposition and philosophical background, possible evidence objections, the testimony of expert witnesses and how the parents present on the witness stand. Rather than obsess about a particular desired outcome or worry about a feared outcome, work with a qualified attorney to prepare rigorously.

To that end, ideally, your lawyer should systematically ask you relevant questions and use your answers to construct a strategy. In our office, for example, we obtain a thorough dossier of information on every client early in the process. We ask clients to complete a 20 page questionnaire. We do this activity not to load up already overwhelmed parents with homework but rather to get insight into what it will take to help them succeed.

This questionnaire gives us a tremendous amount of information, such as where the children go to school, the names of the children's friends, the pediatrician's name, any allergies the children have, and so forth.

The value is twofold. First, the questionnaire lets us measure the client's engagement. If the client returns it with significant incompletions, that response indicates a potentially challenging lack of concern. Secondly, the very process of answering these questions forces parents to appreciate the holistic nature of what needs to be accomplished. That clarity, in turn, translates into a more concrete, achievable set of goals.

For instance, perhaps your son's allergy to cats makes you nervous about allowing him to spend nights with your husband, because his new girlfriend keeps three cats at her apartment. Without this subtle knowledge (obtained via the questionnaire), your attorney would have a hard time negotiating effectively for you and your children.

Many parents wait too far long to hire an attorney and take legal action.

Deferring the process of vetting and hiring a lawyer is understandable, from a psychological perspective. In some ways, it's analogous to why many people with dental pain defer visiting the dentist, despite the obvious risks of doing so.

While few researchers have likely analyzed this question, it would not be surprising to learn that the average parent who divorces contemplates getting separated *hundreds of times* before ever meeting with an attorney. The fears and concerns that paralyze people from taking action are too numerous (and too personal) to itemize, but the consequences are similar and depressing: more money, more time, more anxiety.

When parents wait too long, they cannot go through the ideal process we just outlined. Instead, they must react, often in panicked fashion. In such instances, emergency triage methods may be required. For instance, a parent may need to file an emergency pickup order, which can be very costly.

The other spouse can make the situation worse by using the delay to brainwash the children, siphon funds out of martial accounts, or spend shared assets because of a gambling problem or credit card addiction.

The moral is clear: *file for divorce first*. If you and the other parent reconcile later, you can abandon the process. No one will make you finalize the divorce. If you wait too long, however, expensive fights over things like lawful jurisdiction or relocation could await.

For example, consider two married parents living together in Naples, Florida. One parent decides to separate and move up to Minnesota to live with his family. The children, meanwhile, stay in Naples. The father resides in Minnesota for longer than six months, which means he can file for divorce there if the mother visits Minnesota and is served with divorce papers. This set of circumstances sets the stage for an interstate jurisdictional battle, which leads to extra complexities, costs and logistical problems related to travel. In the worst case scenario, the children move up to Minnesota with the father when the parties separate. Now, Florida has lost jurisdiction over those children, and the whole case has to be fought in Minnesota.

Here is another cautionary tale. One client and his significant other were not married. She was an alcoholic who had been to rehab several times. They had a rocky, on-off relationship. He was jailed four or five times for domestic violence based on untrue, illegitimate allegations. He waited to get legal help until his significant other declared an intention to move to California. She was served the night before she left, so he obtained jurisdiction. However, the emergency process required crisis management on a Saturday night and led to substantial fees. Meanwhile, the mother still took the child to California. The State of Florida issued an emergency pickup order that could not be executed, because he could not even locate the child.

Despite doing everything he could have done per Florida law and done it as quickly as possible and under emergency conditions, he was stuck without good options. His child was somewhere indeterminate in California. No Florida attorney could do much unless the FBI got involved. He eventually had to hire an attorney in California to register the pickup order to try to get it enforced by the California Sheriff's Office. As a direct consequence of his delay in getting started, he had to hire two attorneys and fight twin legal battles on opposite coasts. Thankfully, the story ended well, and he and his son are happily united here in Florida, but it should have never come to this.

How Divorce Related Tumult Affects Children

To respond strategically to help a child, you need empathy. Put yourself in your children's shoes. For instance, consider the example just discussed. Imagine a child who hasn't seen his father in six months and who doesn't know why. Many thoughts might occur to him, such as:

- *Does he not love me anymore?*
- *What did I do wrong?*
- *My mother's always telling me really horrible things about him; he must not be as good as I remembered him to be.*
- *Why was I so wrong to think that he was an okay guy?*

Contentious divorces turn children's worlds upside down. They often must navigate new schools with new children, anxiety and anger regarding missing parents, uncertainty about their home lives, and courtroom battles that leave their parents emotionally drained, financially squeezed and short-tempered. Furthermore, the aftermath of litigation is not always a calm period. Parental relocations, ongoing fighting, and parental alienation can all generate yet more confusion. All and all, divorce for children can be a remarkably disruptive experience with few parallels.

Yet for all that disruption, appreciate that children are resilient. The American Psychological Association, after reviewing recent literature on the subject (apa.org/about/gr/issues/cyf/divorce.aspx), offered the following insights:

"Despite decades of psychological research, there is still considerable debate in the field concerning the effects of divorce on children... Some children do well post-divorce and others do not. However, not enough is known to disentangle the impact of contextual factors that often accompany divorce (e.g., financial pressures and marital conflict) from the impact of the divorce itself…

Key factors that contribute to healthy adjustment post-divorce include appropriate parenting, access to the non-residential parent, custody arrangements, and low parental conflict. Appropriate parenting includes providing emotional support, monitoring children's activities, disciplining authoritatively, and maintaining age-appropriate expectations… the research demonstrates that the best predictor of child adjustment following divorce is the parents' psychological health and the quality of the parent-child relationship."

A Word on Parental Alienation

When divorces grow bitter, many parents engage in unfair and downright unethical practices. One of the worst involves inventing allegations of child abuse or neglect for the purpose of winning a court battle or punishing the other parent. Another terrible practice involves what's technically known as Parental Alienation (PA), the process of brainwashing a child to fear, mistrust or loathe a parent.

Dr. Richard A. Warshak, a respected authority on this topic, defines the problem using this language (warshak.com/publications/what-is-parental-alienation.html):

"Most children whose parents live apart from each other long for a good relationship with both parents and want to be raised by both. In my own studies, and those of other researchers, children say that the worst part of divorce is that they do not get to spend enough time with their parents... The majority of children want contact with both parents on a regular basis, and… [to] balance their time between homes.

Some children, though, do not crave more time with an absent parent. Instead, these children reject one parent, resist contact, or show extreme reluctance to be with the parent. These children are alienated. In some cases, children have good reasons to reject a deficient parent. In other cases, children reject a parent with whom they previously had a good relationship, often paralleling their other parent's negative attitudes. The children's treatment of the rejected parent is disproportionate to that parent's behavior and inconsistent with the prior history of the parent-child relationship."

Parental Alienation is surprisingly common. In our office, we see serious, concerning alienation in probably 20% of cases. Sadly, we see the worst of the worst: the most hotly contested cases. Parental Alienation is (likely) not as high in the common population of all divorces.

The child's behaviors towards the rejected parent are often incredibly hurtful, especially because they're predicated on lies, misinformation and misperception. Bear in mind, however, that the root cause is the spouse's alienation. Consider the child's behaviors and reactions as secondary or symptomatic.

We suggest to our clients that they engage in the painful but necessary work of consistently and visibly maintaining an intention to be involved in the children's lives. Practically speaking, that means giving a gift every holiday as well as a phone call and an *I love you* note. Even if the parent who is watching the children throws these notes away or hides the gifts or deletes your birthday emails, you still want to engage in these activities. If the other parent engages in blatantly debased or unfair behavior, the judge will be much more likely to find alienation and take action on your behalf.

There is no plausible excuse to prevent a child from getting a gift from a loving parent; there is no legitimate way to justify that behavior. We also tell our clients to go to every basketball game, every soccer game, every school music event and other activities of that nature. It is painful to be an alienated parent, but you **must** stick by your children.

In terms of therapies to deal with the alienation and its consequences, consider exploring options like Dr. Richard Warshak's **Family Bridges** program warshak.com/services/family-bridges.html. Described as an "innovative educational and experiential program that helps unreasonably alienated children and adolescents adjust to living with a parent they claim to hate or fear," Family Bridges has also been tested in somewhat rigorous scientific trials.

For instance:

"A study of a larger sample is in progress analyzing data on 88 children who enrolled in the Family Bridges workshop. Thirty-nine of the 88 participants were 14 or older; 26 were 12-13 years old. There were 55 boys and 33 girls. Nearly half of the group of rejected parents are mothers. The preliminary results parallel those found with the smaller sample.

At the workshop's conclusion, 95% of the child participants recovered a positive relationship with the rejected parent. Most of these children previously frustrated the court-ordered parenting plan and threatened to continue to do so if the court did not endorse their stated preferences.... On follow-up, 83% of the sample enjoyed good relationships with the parents they had formerly rejected."

On "Life Balance" and Prioritizing Your Energy During Litigation

Divorce and fights over child custody unquestionably throw life out of balance. Ultimately, you want to stabilize your world and return to healthful, nurturing activities – to get on an exercise program, reboot or advance your career, date and find new, meaningful relationships.

However, appreciate that litigation is not an appropriate time for rebalancing. Commit to your kids and the process, or do not. Prepare yourself for a period of *imbalance*. It will not last forever. The circuit courts strive to resolve every domestic relations case within 12 months. The courts have a directive to get themselves through these cases quickly. The judges follow a rule book that grades them on their efficiency, so they are motivated to move cases through the system.

Different Florida counties work at different speeds. Collier County, for example, has a reputation for moving cases rapidly. Lee County is known for handling matters at a slightly more leisurely pace. The courts work to process litigation fast, because they recognize its disruptive nature both for the parents and also for the children.

Prepare to triage, and put projects on the back burner. After things settle, you will have the opportunity to rebuild. Along those lines, be willing to accept support and financial assistance from friends and families. Many parents operate under the assumption that they must pay their own way and do it all themselves. That attitude is counter-productive. They end up swimming upstream, metaphorically, and they have no time or energy left to be the parents that the court wants them to be.

This urge to "get it all done" comes from a rational and responsible place. You intuitively want to keep your debt modest, rather than letting it increase, for instance. However, prioritizing work over parenting at this juncture could lead to a grimmer outcome by the time trial comes around. If you receive offers of financial help for your litigation from a family member, friend, colleague, employer, or temporary loan source, *take them*. Resist the impulse to dive into work as a means to reassert your autonomy. Instead, prioritize your parenting, and concentrate on the litigation.

Your Posture Towards the Other Parent

The litigation mindset is very different from the mindset you take during alternative dispute resolution (ADR), like mediation. Make no mistake: litigation is a battle. However, be sure to uphold personal standards and values. The court rewards parents who do so. For instance, in Parental Alienation cases, the non-alienating client wins by showing a willingness to communicate; the alienating parent loses by failing to communicate.

Communicating with Your Ex During Litigation

Obviously, be honest, and be kind. Also, avoid unilateral decisions. Even if the decisions seem minor or insignificant, avoid doing things like:

- Enrolling a child in soccer without discussions with your co-parent
- Changing dentists
- Giving the child a dramatic haircut or hairdo style
- Allowing the child to go out late with a boyfriend or to use pushup bras instead of training bras

Any real change in the child's life should be discussed with the other parent, at least inasmuch as you would say *I really want to do X, rather than Y. Can you please give me your thoughts, even if you are indifferent?*

Over communicate. Be diligent and disclosing.

What If You Make a Mistake When Communicating with the Other Parent?

Let's say someone sends you a Facebook message alerting you that your ex is dating your friend. You become angry and send him or her a terrible e-mail. What damage control do you need to do?

Believe it or not, such scenarios occur with some frequency, and they are easily recovered, if the parent doesn't say destructive comments around the child. If you leave a profanity laced voicemail for your ex, and you can hear the child in the background, that voicemail can obviously be problematic evidence. However, private communication between the parents – when the child is not present – is generally less destructive for your case. We are not advocating irresponsible behavior, but you must also forgive yourself for lapses in judgment during this time.

Dating During Divorce Litigation: Rules of Thumb

As we have mentioned, researchers hotly debate the science of how, when and why divorce impacts children, but you need general guidelines. Many trusted psychiatrists say that parents should wait at least six months before introducing a child to a new significant other. The language you use is also important. Avoid calling your new girlfriend "mommy," for instance. Never go into court asking for a parenting plan and use language to the effect of *my girlfriend can pick the kids up from school while I'm at work*. The court will not appreciate that. To the extent that you want to date – and you have the time and energy to do so – go slowly. Go out when you do not have your children with you. Avoid rushing into new relationships.

When you introduce a new person to your children, also introduce him or her to your former significant other. Provide information about the nature of the relationship as well as the person's background. As awkward as this process can be, engage in a conversation among the three of you to lay out ground rules. For example, you might stipulate that you never spank or hit your children. In effect, this new person becomes a part of the family by extension. As such, he or she should follow the house rules.

Here is another scenario to avoid. A husband and wife split up and divorce. The husband finds a new girlfriend; the wife meets a boyfriend. Suddenly, the new girlfriend and boyfriend start co-parenting children who are not their own. The boyfriend and girlfriend communicate between themselves, exchange times and addresses for occasions and complete child care tasks. However, neither one has any legal rights to make decisions for the children. The parents are responsible – or at least, they should be. However, when the spouses don't communicate, or when they communicate poorly, their significant others often come together to fill the void: *somebody's got to communicate; let's just do it ourselves.*

Along those lines, when it comes to using social media, like Facebook and Twitter, use common sense. Avoid posting derisive or diminishing comments about your spouse. Don't add your child to your dating site profile. Do not set up a GoFundMe page to raise money for your litigation. (This advice may seem to contradict earlier guidance to accept money from friends and family to handle your legal battle. However, recognize the big difference between accepting or even actively soliciting money from a parent or friend in private and launching a public, crowdsourced campaign.)

Don't overplay the situation or over dramatize what's happening to you. If you want to create a statement that the court will find genuinely compelling, ask willing friends to testify as witnesses on your behalf. Ideally, they would all tell the court something along the lines of the following: *I knew Alex back when he and his wife were together. He was always so excited and happy to be with his kids. When Alex and his wife separated, and she started keeping the kids from him, he became a mess. He was depressed, and you could tell how being without his kids was tearing him up inside.*

When somebody testifies on your behalf in such a heartfelt, sincere manner, that act means much more than a superficial show of support online.

Divorce During Various Phases of Your Children's Lives

In pregnancy, the major legal challenges come into play if you are unmarried. The pregnancy phase tends to be much more important to paternity cases than to divorce cases. That said, it is a fast moving world, and we often see mothers married to men who are not the fathers of their children. These kinds of scenarios raise big issues that need to be addressed with an attorney.

What about getting divorced while **parenting babies and young kids**? A legal philosophy known as the Tender Years Doctrine used to come into play. The idea, developed and put into practice in England in the 19th century, is that young children (from birth through 4 years of age) need to spend more time with the mother because of attachment and breastfeeding.

However, the courts today in Florida reject this Doctrine. They see no reason, legally, why the father and mother should not have equal parenting time from birth. Instead, they operate under the premise that the state must consider the best interests of the child.

There are a few special considerations, however. For instance, if a mother is breast feeding, then the father should be willing (if in agreement) to use frozen pumped breast milk as necessary and to accommodate working with the new mother on the breastfeeding schedule.

Also, respected psychiatrists have argued that, during the infantile stages, children need to their parents each day. To that end, the court sometimes will order day on, day off arrangements: Monday, mom; Tuesday, dad; Wednesday, mom; Thursday, dad; and so forth. This arrangement leads to a lot of driving, but the children do get to see both parents every day.

In terms of **older kids and teens**, in our practice, we have seen that teens tend to be at greater risk for Parental Alienation. They can align and empathize with the alienating parent more aggressively. One parent, for instance, will allow the teen to do things the other parent will not.

To that end, one parent will almost always want the teenager to testify. To make that happen, the parent needs to file a motion. We have filed quite a few motions along those lines. They are not always granted, but we take action if the client feels it's important to do so. Some practioners have a hard line rule for or against child testimony; we do not. Each case is unique, and the age and maturity of the children as well as the weight of the issues are highly relevant.

Be mindful of the subtle dangers of bringing children into the discussion. Consider the following true story about a divorce that occurred in the 1990s. A brother and sister, both in high school at the time, witnessed their parents go through a miserable divorce involving infidelity and financial mismanagement. The father encouraged both children to testify on his behalf at trial. They did so. Enraged, the mother severed all ties with her children. Later in life, the sister had to deal with a special needs child, a divorce of her own, and painful and scary medical problems. Her mother refused to reach out or offer any assistance, despite the fact that she remarried into great wealth, and she could have easily contributed.

The story illustrates several things:

1. Even seemingly normal people are capable of amazing callousness and bad behavior during divorce.

2. The scars created by the litigation experience can have ramifications for years or decades.

3. Even simple actions – for instance, the father's decision to ask his children to testify – can have unintended consequences.

Obviously, you must move forward with the divorce without benefit of hindsight, but be very mindful about how, when and why you involve your children. Discuss the strategic implications with your attorney first.

When the Other Parent Behaves Unfairly or Engages in Dubious Tactics

Even when you achieve your desired outcomes, litigation can be a painful, personal and depleting process. For example, consider the following true situation. A client's wife had accused him of being a drug user and an alcoholic. She had no witnesses to support her position, no pictures and no evidence. Yet the client had to hire a counselor to evaluate him and to testify that he was clean and that he had no substance abuse issues. The client also had to have his mother and his sister testify to that end. All rational arguments aside, however, the trial still thematically focused on the client's "substance abuse issues" (or lack thereof) and thus potentially affected the judge's subconscious perceptions.

The moral here is that the mere act of leveling an accusation, even an untrue or absurd one, flavors the discussion. It creates an anchor in people's minds that colors their interpretation of the facts. Your attorney must then exert careful effort to set the record straight in both the logical/rational frame and the emotional/subconscious frame. That takes a lot of work.

This case raises a key theme of this book: ***if and when possible, strive to avoid litigation. Find another way forward.***

Can you swallow certain unpleasant compromises? Can you find it in you to be kind to a former spouse, despite what he has put you through? Can you budget to pay more than you feel is fair for child support or alimony, just in the name of bringing peace to the situation?

Obviously, you want to avoid compromising on key issues related to property division and to your children. However, appreciate the toll that litigation takes; be mindful of its costs and the tradeoffs you make.

SECTION FOUR

HOW TO SELECT THE RIGHT FAMILY LAW ATTORNEY FOR YOUR NEEDS

To give real service you must add something which cannot be bought or measured with money, and that is sincerity and integrity.

– Douglas Adams

If you are stuck with litigation as your only or best alternative, you need an attorney with tremendous experience and focus in this area – somebody who handles this type of work exclusively and all the time. That is essential.

If you wait too long or opt for middling representation, less than ideal outcomes will follow. Maybe your ex-spouse will prevent you from seeing your child or offer only every other weekend visitation. Work with somebody who understands divorce issues and who knows:

- Exactly what type of evidence the judge wants to see
- The level and purpose of all communication required of you
- The factors that the court considers when evaluating families

As we have discussed, avoid waiting too long to retain legal help. Many clients decide to engage the services of a family lawyer when they are metaphorically already hurtling to the ground. Fumbling for the parachute at that late hour is a recipe for anxiety and bad results.

Process for Finding and Vetting a Family Law Firm

First of all, determine your values and priorties for the relationship. To articulate these and use them as criteria when choosing your attorney, try the following exercise. Fill in the blanks below:

I would allow anyone to choose my attorney, as long as that person...

____

____

____

____

The answers you write down might be along the lines of the following:

- *The attorney is no more than 30 minutes from my house.*
- *The attorney has successfully handled at least a dozen cases similar to my situation.*
- *The law firm's staff seems organized and responsive.*
- *I get a "good vibe" from my preliminary conversations with the team.*

Next, cast a relatively wide net to assess candidate law firms. Use personal references, internet investigations and other means to create a "short list" of candidates. Use your criteria (developed in the exercise above) to winnow your list further, and then arrange consultations with the top candidates.

During your consultations, ask detailed, probing questions, and write down the answers that you get. Be comprehensive. For instance:

- What inspires you and your team to do the work you do? What are your values?
- What experience do you have handling cases similar to mine?

- What specific qualifications do you have with respect to Florida family law?
- Why *shouldn't* someone hire your firm?
- What expectations do you have for clients?
- What are your biggest weaknesses?
- Based on my story, what strategic approach might you initially suggest?
- How does your fee structure work?
- Etc.

Once you colect all this information, reflect. Rationally assess the candidates and compare them, and also pay attention to your gut intuition. Our subconscious minds are very good at picking up small but vital details that our conscious minds often ignore. So rely on your head *and* your heart to choose your attorney. (If you find that you're still struggling after all this work and research, try this useful decision making trick, lifehacker.com/follow-your-gut-and-make-better-decisions-with-this-sim-1214011055)

Be wary of a one size fits all approach to your matter. Some cases do not go to Court. Others need only a referral to an A+ counselor. Don't allow your attorney to "make" you do something. We always say: *we hold the map, but you hold the wheel.*

Why Us: Why People Choose Our Team to Handle Their Divorce Litigation

1. Our passion and sense of purpose

My personal attachment to family law runs deep, because of my biography and my own relationship with my family. While other areas of the law interest me intellectually, they don't compel the fire and sense of mission that family law does. Every person on the team feels this passion. We have all been touched by family law issues.

Our senior attorney has been divorced, and his kids were devastated by the process. Our legal assistant is a step parent adoptee. As a child, I was stepparent adopted at age 5, and my Dad is my hero. My wife left her house when she was 15, and there have been many ups and downs with her parents for years.

Everybody in the country has some family law backstory, depending on how deeply you probe. Divorce, adoption, abuse/ neglect and intergenerational conflict universally affect us. That said, in our office, we feel a particularly strong bond to our work because of our personal histories.

2. Our tested systems and processes that we are always improving.

We are singularly focused on improving our processes to ensure quality and to reduce costs for our clients, while making their lives better. We are constantly improving what we do – constantly changing and improving our videos, our forums, our questionnaires, and beyond. Every thing our firm and our business does gets better as a result of this drive towards continual self-reflection and self-improvement.

At our firm, we're passionate about processes and systems. In our experience, attention to these details helps our clients achieve their outcomes and gives them peace of mind.

In addition to questionnaires, for instance, we provide videos about how to complete the financial affidavit. Our clients enjoy our videos, because they save them time and stress. They can watch them whenever they want, and the tutorials explain complex legal processes in plain, easy to understand language. They also cover a host of frequently asked questions.

After a parent completes the questionnaire, our paralegal reviews it with him or her and then sets up a case strategy meeting with the attorney assigned to the file. The attorney also reviews the questionnaire and the financial affidavit and asks more questions, such as:

- Whom do we need to subpoena?
- What do we need to subpoena?
- What do we need to prove at trial?

- What are the client's goals and objectives?
- How will we get there?
- What interrogatives, requests for production, and depositions do we need to take?
- What motions do we need to file?

The attorneys meticulously gather information to establish the roadmap for the case, and the rest of our team executes this plan.

3. **Our honesty and integrity.**

The only thing you can control in litigation is your own word. You can't control what anyone else will do, and we are in absolute, unequivocal alignment on this value. I have seen lawyers lie in court, and I know for a fact they are lying. Everyone knows they are. We do not accept or condone that kind of behavior. We will never lie in court. It doesn't matter if a client wants to pay a billion dollars – that will not happen. It's right in our retainer: you have to be honest with us, because we will be honest with you.

I have lost many potential cases because I have told prospective clients *you're probably looking at a $20,000 case if it goes to trial.* I could have easily sold them on our services if I had underplayed the costs. However, then they would end up dissatisfied, and/or we simply would not be able to provide the services needed to reach their goals. The costs in our office are a reflection of the tools and resources we employ to prove our cases at trial.

CONCLUSION

"Sometimes the best and worst times of your life can coincide. It is a talent of the soul to discover the joy in pain—thinking of moments you long for, and knowing you'll never have them again. The beautiful ghosts of our past haunt us, and yet we still can't decide if the pain they caused us out weighs the tender moments when they touched our soul. This is the irony of love."
– Shannon L. Adler

Unfortunately, no one can undo the hurt and pain of your separation, nor can you rapidly and easily handle all the challenges of litigation and the child custody and visitation battles ahead. However, this book hopefully has given you critical insights into what to expect, what to do and what to avoid doing to get the outcome you hope to achieve and to be the parent you want to be during this time.

We began by exploring practical tips for parenting while going through a strenuous separation. Next, we catalogued diverse resources for parents in Florida to manage their needs and their children's needs. In our third chapter, we unpacked key ideas about Florida divorce law and litigation and discussed practical tips for how to approach a contentious separation. Finally, we examined the process of searching for family law attorneys and offered a systematic way to assess candidate law firms.

We hope this book has given you clarity about your situation and some hope. Remember: *you will get through this period of your life*. Cultivate forgiveness, determination and empathy; but most of all, learn to love yourself for who you are, fully and completely. Our team at Family First Legal Group is standing by to offer a confidential strategic consultation at 239-206-3664. We also have many more resources available at familyfirstlegalgroup.com. Please reach out to get the help you deserve.

DISCLAIMER

Disclaimer for "The Florida Parent's Divorce Handbook: How to Protect Your Rights, So You Can Protect Your Kids"

You understand that this book is not intended as a substitution for a consultation with an attorney. Requesting this book or viewing the information in it does not create an attorney-client relationship with Family First Legal Group or any of its attorneys. To obtain legal advice about your Florida divorce, please engage the services of Family First Legal Group or another law firm of your choice. To discuss engaging Family First Legal Group to help you with your matter, please contact the firm.

FAMILY FIRST LEGAL GROUP IS PROVIDING "THE FLORIDA PARENT'S DIVORCE HANDBOOK: HOW TO PROTECT YOUR RIGHTS, SO YOU CAN PROTECT YOUR KIDS" (HEREAFTER REFERRED TO AS "BOOK") AND ITS CONTENTS ON AN "AS IS" BASIS AND MAKES NO REPRESENTATIONS OR WARRANTIES OF ANY KIND WITH RESPECT TO THIS BOOK OR ITS CONTENTS. FAMILY FIRST LEGAL GROUP DISCLAIMS ALL SUCH REPRESENTATIONS AND WARRANTIES, INCLUDING FOR EXAMPLE WARRANTIES OF MERCHANTABILITY AND FITNESS FOR A PARTICULAR PURPOSE. IN

ADDITION, FAMILY FIRST LEGAL GROUP DOES NOT REPRESENT OR WARRANT THAT THE INFORMATION ACCESSIBLE VIA THIS BOOK IS ACCURATE, COMPLETE OR CURRENT.

The book is provided for information purposes only, and relevant laws frequently change. Neither Family First Legal Group nor any authors, contributors, or other representatives will be liable for damages arising out of or in connection with the use of this book. This is a comprehensive limitation of liability that applies to all damages of any kind, including (without limitation) compensatory; direct, indirect or consequential damages; loss of data, income or profit; loss of or damage to property, and claims of third parties and punitive damages.

Made in the USA
Monee, IL
04 November 2026

67387900R00046